Ann Ingalls
Maria Corte Maidagan

J IS FOR
JAZZ

BRIGHT
connections media

A World Book Encyclopedia Company

Note to the reader: In J Is for Jazz, you will find
some words and phrases that may be unfamiliar to
you, such as "gig" and "gnat's whistle." You will find
such words and phrases defined in the glossary in the
back of the book.

J Is for Jazz
Print ISBN: 978-1-62267-026-0

BRIGHT CONNECTIONS MEDIA is a trademark of World Book, Inc.

Bright Connections Media
A World Book Encyclopedia Company
233 North Michigan Avenue, Suite 2000
Chicago, Illinois 60601
U.S.A.

For information about other BCM publications, visit our website at
www.brightconnectionsmedia.com, or call 1-800-967-5325.

Printed in China by Toppan Leefung Printing Ltd.,
Guangdong Province
1st printing July 2014

J IS FOR
JAZZ

BRIGHT
connections media

A World Book Encyclopedia Company

The Story of Jazz!

Jazz is a kind of music that began in the United States in the late 1800's. Jazz grew from a mixture of different kinds of music, including black American music and African rhythms.

Jazz musicians often make up music as they play it. Musicians call this improvisation. Improvisation is part of what makes jazz different from other kinds of music. It makes the person who plays the music the person who creates it. Another important part of jazz is called syncopation. In syncopation, the musical patterns are uneven and the musical notes are accented, or stressed, in unusual places.

Jazz may be performed by a single musician or by a small group of musicians called a combo. Sometimes it is performed by a band of 10 or more musicians. Many instruments are used to play jazz. Brass instruments used to play jazz include the trumpet and the slide trombone. Reed instruments include the clarinet and saxophone. Other instruments include the piano, drums, and bass. Guitar is also used in some types of jazz.

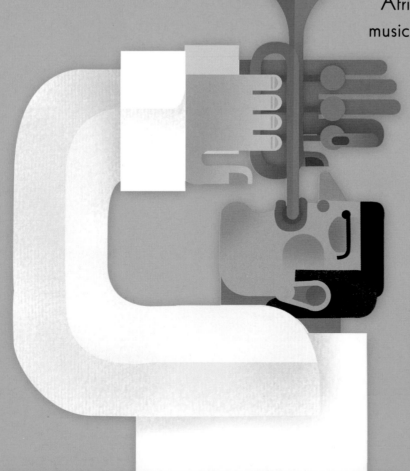

The earliest jazz was performed by African Americans who had not studied music formally. They listened to ragtime, a type of music popular in the late 1800's and early 1900's that has great energy and syncopation. They also listened to the blues, a sad kind of music with much repetition. They listened to band music played at African American funerals and in parades. And they knew many folk songs and pieces of dance music. From all these types of music, jazz was born. Jazz probably started in New Orleans in the early 1900's. Today, this style of jazz music is called Dixieland Jazz.

In time, other types of jazz came about. The decade of the 1920's is often called the golden age of jazz or the Jazz Age. Jazz spread from New Orleans to other American cities, such as Memphis, St. Louis, Kansas City, Chicago, Detroit, and New York City. It began to be played on the radio. Jazz stayed popular after this golden age. In the 1930's, big bands formed with both black and white musicians. Jazz singers sang popular songs. Many people, both black and white, enjoyed the bands and the singers and danced to the music.

Swing jazz was popular with the big bands of the 1930's. It had its own special rhythm. The name "swing" came from the song "It Don't Mean a Thing If It Ain't Got That Swing," which was recorded in 1932 by Duke Ellington.

In the 1940's, bebop was a new jazz style. It was a difficult style, and the musicians who played it had great skill. Each phrase, or part, of the music had many notes and many surprises. Cool jazz, popular in the 1940's and 1950's, had a soft sound. Hard bop, in the 1950's, added blues music and church music to jazz.

In the 1970's, fusion jazz became popular. It combined jazz with rock music. Some jazz musicians used electronic instruments, and some even used computers to create new sounds.

Today, many styles of jazz are popular. Many musicians play swing and bebop. Others play fusion jazz. Electronic technology is also being used more in jazz music today.

Now you know some of the history of the marvelous music known as jazz!

Learn more by enjoying J Is for Jazz!

A is for America's Music.
It ab-so-tive-ly began with
African American rhythms.
And how!

B is for Blues, the heart of jazz.

Its sad, simple sound helped give jazz its flavor. Some of the best jazz cats have been hip to the blues!

C is for Count Basie, the jazz pianist and songwriter.

The Count said, "If you play a tune and a person don't tap their feet, don't play the tune."

D is for the Duke—Edward Kennedy Ellington.

This unreal pianist and composer played more than 20,000 gigs! He got his nickname because he was such a sharp dresser.

Duke was one ducky Daddy-o!

E is for Ella Fitzgerald, "the First Lady of Song."

In 1934, she belted out a melody at the Apollo Theatre in New York City's Harlem neighborhood and won a contest.

Lady Ella was the elephant's eyebrows!

F is for Floorflushers.

They just couldn't stop their dogs from dancing to this jumping music.

They put on their glad rags and got a wiggle on!

G is for Benny Goodman, "The King of Swing."

As a 10-year-old in short pants in Chicago, he played the clarinet to make pocket change. When this jazzman picked up his licorice stick, he could really groove.

Swing, Benny, swing!

H is for Horns.

Saxophones, cornets, trombones, trumpets, and clarinets. Brassy, sassy cats with balloon lungs required.

Honey, no jazz band is hip to the jive without the sweet sounds of horns.

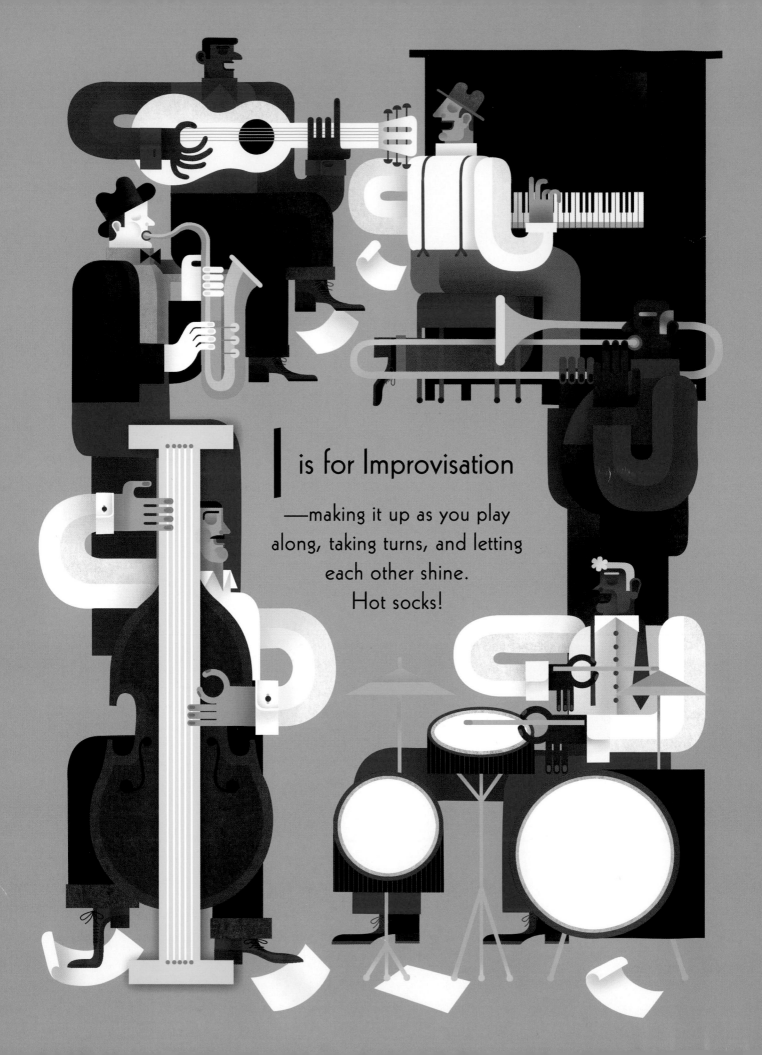

I is for Improvisation

—making it up as you play
along, taking turns, and letting
each other shine.
Hot socks!

J is for Jelly Roll Morton.

This jazz pianist and his band, the Red Hot Peppers, shaped the sound of jazz by mixing up ragtime and the blues.

Jelly Roll and his music could really shine—just like the diamond in his front tooth!

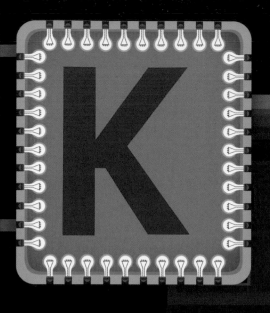

MAJESTIC

THE CHERRY BLOSSOM

JAZZ CLUB

RENO CLUB

K is for Kansas City,
"the heavenly city."

Cats played and sang at more than 50 different venues—
the Blue Room, the Reno Club, the Jungle Room, the
Drum Room, the Cherry Blossom, and the Majestic.

KC was the bee's knees!

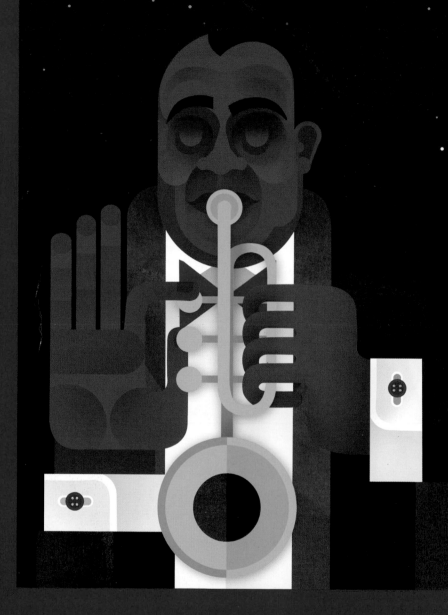

L is for Louis "Satchmo" Armstrong.

"Born poor, died rich, and never hurt anyone along the way," said the Duke about his buddy. Satchmo is famous for tru and cornet playing and jazz singing.

Scat cat!

M is for Miles Davis.

In 1945, he went to New York City to study
music at the Juilliard School. But he spent most
of his time blowing trumpet with jazz bands.

He was one cool cat!

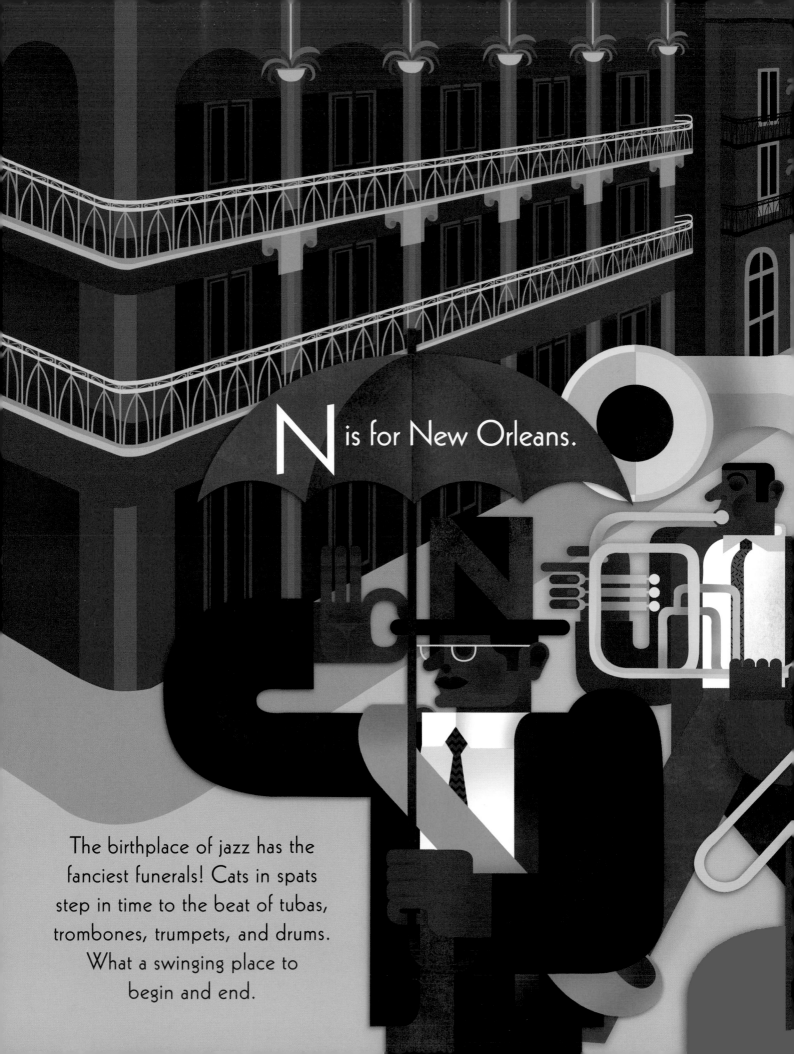

N is for New Orleans.

The birthplace of jazz has the
fanciest funerals! Cats in spats
step in time to the beat of tubas,
trombones, trumpets, and drums.
What a swinging place to
begin and end.

O is for the Original Dixieland Jazz Band, the first jazz band
to make phonograph records with music that young rug-cutters really dug!

Q is for Quartets and Quintets, combos of four or five musicians playing drums, sax, trumpet, cornet, bass, trombone, piano, guitar, or vibes.

Listen to those cats frisking the whiskers before the big jam session!

R is for Ragtime, all the rage before jazz.

Scott Joplin, "the King of Ragtime," named his composition the "Maple Leaf Rag" for the Maple Leaf Club in Sedalia, Missouri, where he jammed on the piano in the 1890's.

He pos-i-lute-ly percolated.

S is for Spirituals. Clap, sway, raise the roof and rattle the rafters!

T is for Thelonious Monk,
who put on the Ritz with dazzling drapes and funny hats.

Monk got up from the piano in the middle of
tickling the ivories and moved to the groove.

Solid!

U is for Uptown, Upbeat, Upscale, and Urban.

Jazz busts out in cities, hotels, and restaurants.
Owls get gigs and jam for some jack!

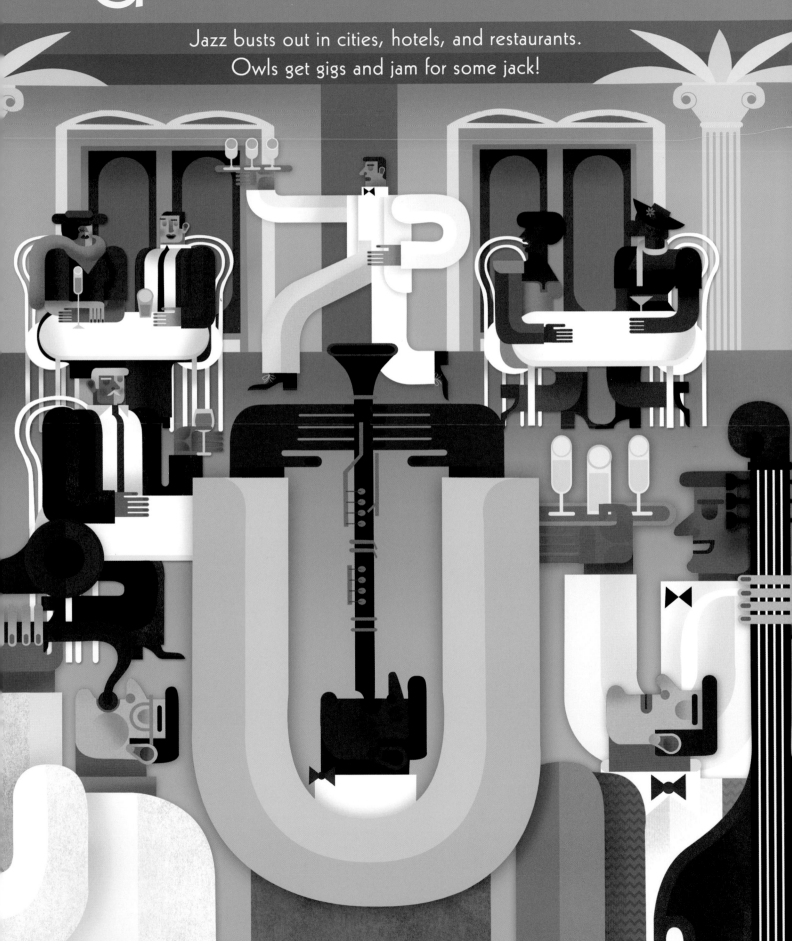

V is for Vibes, short for Vibraphone, a percussion instrument with metal bars that echo. Lionel Hampton made this instrument sing.

W is for Mary Lou Williams, "the Boogie-Woogie Queen."

This "lady who liked to swing the band" played music with one hand and wrote it for the next act with the other.

Soul on soul!

X is for aXe.

Every jazz musician has a favorite axe that is exactly right.

Musicians try to hit on all sixes with their axe! Boom-cha-ka, plinkety, tic-bam-cling!

Y is for Lester "Prez" Young, who could make a note anywhere on his sax because of fancy fingering. Yowza!

And he made up a silly language, calling his fingers "people" and practice, a "molly trolley." You slay me, Prez!

Z is for Zoot Suits.

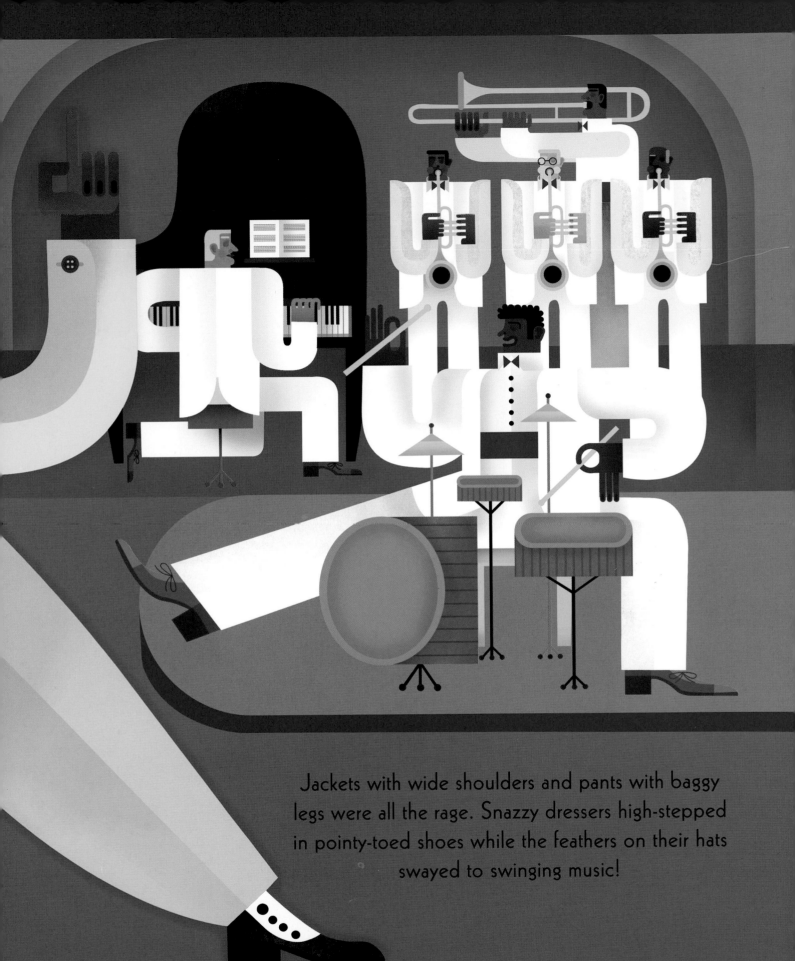

Jackets with wide shoulders and pants with baggy
legs were all the rage. Snazzy dressers high-stepped
in pointy-toed shoes while the feathers on their hats
swayed to swinging music!

Glossary of Jazz Slang

And how!: I strongly agree!

Axe: Instrument.

Balloon lungs: A brass instrument player who can hold a note for a long time.

Bebop: A complicated rhythmic, melodic, and harmonic type of jazz that developed in the 1940's.

Bee's knees: Terrific!

Big cheese: An important person.

Bounce: A happy musical beat.

Break it down!: Get hot! Go to town!

Canary: A female singer.

Cat: Jazz musician or jazz fan.

Cat's meow, Cat's pajamas, or **Cat's whiskers**: Great!

Chirp: Sing.

Combo: A small group of musicians.

Daddy-o: One hipster greeting another.

Dogs: Feet.

Drapes: Dress-up clothes.

Ducky: Very good.

Elephant's eyebrows: Terrific!

Finger zinger: A musician who plays an instrument very fast.

Floorflusher: A person who loves to dance.

Frisking the whiskers: Warming up before a session.

Get a wiggle on: Get going.

Gig: A job playing music.

Gimme some skin, Hand me some skin, or **Slip me some skin**: Shake hands.

Glad rags: Dress-up clothes.

Gnat's whistle: Terrific!

Groovy: Music that really swings.

High hat: A snob.

Hip: To know or to understand.

Hip to the jive: Really cool or trendy.

Hipster: A person who is cool.

Hit on all sixes: To perform to the best of one's abilities.

Hot dawg! or **Hot socks!**: Great!

Humdinger: A person, thing, action, or statement of remarkable excellence or effect.

Ivories: The keys of a piano.

Jack: Money.

Jam: Hot playing.

Jive: To play swing music or early jazz.

Joe: Coffee.

Jump: To have a good time.

Licorice stick: A clarinet.

Lollapalooza: A person, thing, action, or statement of remarkable excellence or effect.

Mop: A handkerchief.

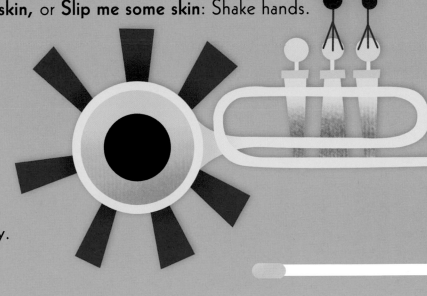
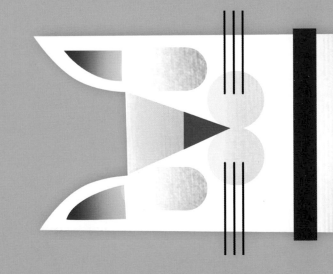

Owl: A person who stays out late.

Percolate: Music that runs smoothly or "perks."

Pipe down: Stop talking.

Pos-i-lute-ly!: Absolutely! Positively! Yes!

Putting on the Ritz: To dress very stylishly.

Razz: To make fun of.

Rug-cutter: A dancer.

Scat: To sing with rhythmic sounds instead of words.

Short pants: Knee-length trousers that were worn by boys during the late 1800's to early 1900's.

Sinker: A donut.

Skins: The drums.

Solid!: Excellent!

Squeak box: Violin.

Squeeze box: Accordion.

Stilts: Legs.

Swing: To play lively jazz music.

Unreal: Special.

Wail: To play very well.

Wax a disk: To record a song.

What's eating you?: What's wrong?

Woodshed: To practice.

You slay me!: That's funny!

Yowza!: Wow!

Zoot suit: Exaggerated clothing.